Paris

Books by Richard Jones

Paris
Avalon
Stranger on Earth
The Obscure Hours: Translations
The King of Hearts
The Correct Spelling & Exact Meaning
Apropos of Nothing
The Blessing: New & Selected Poems
The Stone It Lives On
48 Questions
The Abandoned Garden
A Perfect Time
At Last We Enter Paradise
Sonnets
Country of Air
Walk On
Innocent Things
Windows and Walls

Paris
RICHARD JONES

A Tebot Bach Book

Tebot Bach
P.O. Box 7887
Huntington Beach, CA 92615
ww.TebotBach.org

Paris

Printed on recycled paper in the United States of America.

ISBN: 9781939678706

Book design by Madelyn Funk and Sabrina Szos.
Text set in Adobe Garamond Pro & Gill Sans.
Cover art: *A Wallace Fountain*, photograph by Richard Jones.

A Tebot Bach Book

Tebot Bach, Welsh for little teapot, is a Nonprofit Public Benefit Corporation, which sponsors workshops, forums, lectures, and publications. Tebot Bach books are distributed by Small Press Distribution, Armadillo, and Ingram.

The Tebot Bach Mission: Advancing literacy, strengthening community, and transforming life experiences with the power of poetry through readings, workshops, and publications.

Acknowledgments

AGNI: "At the Carnavalet and the Cognacq-Jay," *"Christ in the Garden of Olives"*

American Literary Review: "Dalí"

The Apple Valley Review: *"The Golden Sphere,"* "The Place des Vosges," "Surrealism"

Asheville Poetry Review: "Brancusi," "Rilke and Rodin"

BOAAT: "The Flâneur," "The French Word for 'Sky,'" "Gustave Moreau"

Cimarron Review: "Tin Cups"

Columbia Poetry Review: "Cathedral"

The Comstock Review: "Aura"

Cultural Weekly: "George Whitman," "Redouté," "Sonnet"

Escape into Life: "Je t'aime," "Notre-Dame"

The Hamilton Stone Review: "The Bateau-Lavoir," "The Drunken Boat," "The Gift," "The Left Bank," "Letter to a Friend," *"The Water Lilies: Green Reflections"*

Image: "Pont des Arts"

The Magnolia Review: "Strindberg and Miller"

One: *"Achilles Mourning the Death of Patroclus"*

Rhino: "Baudelaire"

Smartish Pace: "Existential"

Southern Poetry Review: "Courbet"

Some Paris poems appeared in *The Blessing: New & Selected Poems* and *Stranger on Earth,* both from Copper Canyon Press.

Contents

for the bouquinistes

my head is so far up in the clouds
that I can imagine all of us
are angels in paradise

—written on the wall
at Shakespeare and Company

Paris

Rilke and Rodin

In Meudon is
Auguste Rodin's hilltop home,
and I'm sitting on the lawn in the warm sun,
doing a little work with my pen and notebook
at a green, round, wrought-iron table
much like the table I have back home.
I'm wondering what it was like to be sensitive young Rilke,
the great master's secretary,
watching the old sculptor with his chisel and mallet.
In their day, these hills were farms and vineyards.
Horse carts climbed the slopes to deliver stone,
and carriages brought customers to see the sculptures.
Rose and Camille vied for Rodin's attention,
his affection, but Rodin told Rilke,
Rien que travailler.
Work. That was the key.
Rilke envied Rodin's ability to rescue
inwardness from stone,
inwardness
the poet wanted to achieve with words,
though he had yet to find a way.
Rodin told Rilke
that before he could ever hope to make a poem
he must first learn to see.
That was the secret. *Secrets and keys,*
I write in my notebook, then doodle some lines,
which become trees on the distant hills.
I draw an eye in the empty sky, then another eye,
then fill two pages with all-seeing eyes.
Du mußt dein Leben ändern.
The ancients believed thought and intellection
resided not in the head, the place of the crown,

but in the torso where we feel things,
the heart bright as the sun in its rib cage.
When a god looks at you with his true vision, Rilke said,
there is no place to hide.
Rilke believed, as I do now, in illumination,
the astonishment of transformation,
but the lost, dark young man who read Rilke's poems
believed *he* needed to change his life
every day, like a shirt.
Sitting at the green iron table
surrounded by the flowering forsythia,
I see Rodin's gardens are not unlike my own.
I have no view of Paris
or paths of crushed stone that ramble
down a terraced hillside through vineyards,
but still I miss my own Meudon,
my lawn and white birdhouses,
the sparrows and finches
that sing in my spruces and maples.
The sad fact that Rodin had no cherry trees
inspires a fondness
for the tender way my cherry trees
reach down and comfort me
as I dream at my table
while my children swing in the hammock
and light plays with time through the leaves.
This morning when I woke
in the dark of a tiny Paris apartment,
I couldn't have imagined
a place like the Villa des Brillants,
but now that I'm here,
writing in my notebook at a table on the lawn,
I see how familiar it all is, how much like home.
Looking at the artist's steeply gabled redbrick house,

I half expect to see my wife open the high bedroom window
and in a flowing nightgown lean out—
her hair disheveled and wild—
calling down in French to ask
what I'm doing
and would I like to come upstairs.
She knows perfectly well I'm working,
that I've found the secret, the key,
but she also knows I'll close my notebook
and climb the stairs to join her.

Baudelaire

Aragon noted
how men love to linger
on the threshold of their imagination.

"Before I compose a piece," said Erik Satie,
"I walk around it several times,
accompanied by myself."

Hemingway said he would cross the bridge
to the Île de la Cité and walk along the quais
when he was trying to think something out.

Baudelaire claimed he would take long strolls,
and find himself everywhere
at home.

Rimbaud said that one must be
a seer who reads signs
of wonder.

Leonardo wrote in his notebooks:
"Pay attention in the street towards evening,
when the weather is bad."

"The apparition of these faces in the crowd;
petals on a wet, black bough,"
Pound said.

During his surrealist period
Giacometti sculpted only those objects
inspired by the "interior model."

The fox says to the little prince,
"What is essential
is invisible to the eye."

And then tonight,
walking home from the cafés of the Bastille,
on a florist's windowglass that framed an enormous red flower

I saw, painted in fluid white cursive, a line by Romain Gary,
*"N'ayez pas peur d'être heureux,
c'est juste un bon moment à passer."*

Don't be afraid to be happy,
even this sweet moment
is passing.

Yesterday, at the Hôtel de Ville, I saw
children skating on the ice rink
even though spring is almost here and it's warm

and the ice beneath the children
was melting into clear pools
and it looked like they were skating on water.

Je t'aime.

I wasn't in Paris in 2015.
I was home in my own Meudon,

lying in a cold hammock, listening
to the winter birds preach

about poetry,

shivering and wondering,
as I often do, about death…

but then came the news—
the sacrilege

of slaughtering writers
gathered around a table to think

and talk. And the autumn night
of the Bataclan massacre—

I wasn't there, either.

Had I been in Paris,
I'd probably have been in Saint-Chapelle,

listening to a concert of Chopin or Satie
and dreaming about beauty,

even after stopping to open my knapsack of books
for the security guard to search.

The execution of writers enraged me.

After Bataclan, I sobbed for days,
knowing all of Paris had been violated.

It's one thing to ponder death and beauty,
but today beauty is under siege and death

is everywhere. *Ubiquiste. Omniprésent.*
When teaching Shakespeare's sonnets

or asking my students to help me understand
the irresistible charm of Renoir's paintings,

I always keep an eye on our classroom door—

the only way in, the only way out.
When my wife and daughter and

I ride bikes to the crowded
farmers' market and buy gladioluses

from the smiling lady
in the white tent, I'm relieved

we all come home alive.

When late at night
I think about Paris,

what keeps me awake
is the irreversible truth:

a dozen intellectuals
and ninety concertgoers

did not at day's end lie down
in their beds and whisper

in the close dark
to the ones they loved,

Bonne nuit. Beaux rêves.
Je t'aime.

The Flâneur

On Saturday morning I rise early
and take the metro to the Marmottan
to see the new Impressionist show,
Les Impressionnistes en privé,
with paintings by Renoir and Pissarro
and one hundred rarely shown masterpieces
from private collections.
A light rain is falling
as I turn the big key in the old lock,
descend the apartment's curved staircase,
open my umbrella and hurry down the narrow street
to the Saint-Paul station,
thinking about the paintings,
thinking about Sisley, Cézanne, and Degas,
feeling breathless, feeling as if I were freshly in love
and on my way to a secret rendezvous.
Yet forty-five minutes later,
when I come up out of the metro at Muette
and begin walking in the Auteuil,
the now-elegant neighborhood
where Marcel Proust was born,
the Ranelagh Gardens are so lovely in the rain
that I linger an hour,
taking pictures of the forsythia
and the cherry trees in bloom.
In the distance I spy a Wallace fountain
and cross the street to take its picture,
the four Graces bathed by the rain
and glistening beneath the dripping elms.
When I finally get to the Marmottan,
the stately mansion devoted to Monet's paintings,
the line is already two blocks long—

a long weekend line.
"A two-and-a-half-hour wait,"
the last man in line informs me.
The gentleman is tall, elegant, wearing a tweed cap,
and the shoulders of his coat are dark with rain.
His shoes are wet and look cold.
I take a long breath. I look down the block
at the queue turning the first corner
and trailing on, unmoving, to the next.
I want to tell the Parisians waiting in the long, damp line
that I admire their patience and devotion,
their willingness to stand in the rain
under their black umbrellas
on a chilly Saturday:
it shows how much they love their Impressionists,
how much they love their artists
and their museums.
But standing under my umbrella
with plump drops dribbling from the edge,
I remind myself that I'm not a Parisian.
I'm just a tourist
free to come next week
and it might be wise
to avoid looking over crowds of shoulders to see.
I'll come early Tuesday morning, I reason,
when I'll have the museum to myself.
I've waited all my life—
what's three more days? Monet will still be here.
My mind weighs the questions
and resolves to let the day take me where it will,
"somewhere i have never travelled,
gladly beyond,"
as E. E. Cummings once put it.
I step out of the line—

already thirty others have joined in behind me—
and stroll away down avenue Raphael,
a free man, a flâneur out for the day,
walking in the drizzle, going slow,
taking the time to look at everything.
The neighborhood is one of embassies and consulates,
mansions and private gardens.
Outside the residence
of Madagascar's ambassador,
the bars of the tall black-iron fence
are just wide enough apart
for the lens of my curious camera.
Maybe I'll find a chameleon climbing the garden wall
or a lemur sitting on the rail of the balcony?
The rain lets up a little.
The Indian ambassador's house
is made rich with bright red shutters
while the Italian Consulate General
boasts an Alfa Romeo 159 in the circular drive.
Walking slowly, stopping to take pictures,
now and then over the rooftops I see
the very top of the Eiffel Tower,
the aerial antenna and cupola.
It almost seems the tower is peeking at me,
flirting maybe,
a little shyly at first,
but then as I round the corner,
the entire latticed beauty steps toward me—
perfectly framed at the end of the boulevard,
the clouds parting behind her,
the sun making her shine.
Love-struck, smitten,
I dawdle on the esplanade at the Trocadero—
riveted, spellbound.

In my mind the tower's airy essence mingles
with all the books I've been reading this week,
the recollected noise of my typewriter,
the smells of my kitchen,
and just as T.S. Eliot wrote in his essay
on "The Metaphysical Poets,"
I experience something new—
something that makes me feel whole and complete.
Though I've seen the tower a thousand times before,
when I cross the Seine
I don't know whether to just stand on the bridge
and admire her charms
or to take her winsome picture yet again.
I make my way quickly through thick crowds
to the end of the winding ticket line,
then shoulder-to-shoulder with a host of others
climb the winding stairs,
stopping to catch my breath
and chat with honeymooners from Virginia—
I smile to hear the English roots of their Tidewater accents,
the way they glide over their vowels
or like my father say *Paah-ris* and *Aa-full Tow-uh*—
and then talk to a man from Amsterdam
who tells me he comes every spring to France
and faithfully climbs the tower.
On the windblown viewing platform,
I am handed a camera and politely asked in sign language
to take a photo—four teenaged girls from Japan
with polka-dot backpacks and souvenir T-shirts.
I close one eye.
Behind the girls' faces,
behind their blowing, silken hair,
I coincidentally, though perfectly, frame
the distant hills of Montmartre

and the white basilica of Sacré-Cœur.
They laugh as I snap a picture,
plus one for good luck
and one for eternity.
When I hand the camera back,
I smile and bow,
and they smile and bow,
not knowing the Sacred Heart of Paris will now
forever look upon them
and bless them.
I walk the observation deck alone and at ease,
separating myself out,
as I sometimes do in crowded museums,
when I wait for the rooms to clear
so I can look at a painting up close, undisturbed.
A little tired, I lean back against the ironwork
to rest and look west—
the sky painted with dark, racing clouds
and sudden shards of sunlight
falling on the rooftops of the Auteuil
and the lines of Impressionist-loving Parisians.
And beyond the Marmottan, on the far horizon,
the green forests of the Bois de Boulogne.
I've not yet been to the Bois de Boulogne,
and from this great height and distance
I can't see the English-styled gardens
and picturesque lakes I've read about
or the winding paths I've only seen on postcards.
Standing high in the tower with the Paris wind,
I think of Marcel Proust walking those gardens as a child,
trailing a little behind his parents,
his mind secretly taking in every detail—
every leaf, raindrop, and blossom,
his mother's and his father's every word.

Brancusi

I cross the rain-slick cobblestone plaza
in front of the Pompidou Center
and go down a dozen blue slate steps
to a low building hidden from the street—
Constantin Brancusi's reconstructed atelier.
I close my umbrella and step inside,
saying hello to the guard and the lady at the desk,
who recognize me from my visits all week.
They nod as I continue around the corner
to a passageway that circles the studio
allowing visitors to look through panes of glass
at the artist's world and the life he lived,
the studio with its white walls, floor, and ceiling.
In the corridor I take off my raincoat,
then take a moment to let my hands warm up.
A group of students on a bench, *élèves*,
listen as their teacher reads from the brochure:
"Brancusi saw the artist
as an intercessor who reveals
the cosmic essence of the material."
My eye roams over the many sculptures,
the austere shapes bearing no hint of abstraction.
Toward the end of his life,
Brancusi could no longer bear
to sell his sculptures or even part with them.
He believed they were most understood
in groupings arranged in the studio
where they were created,
alongside his sketches and tools,
mallets and chisels,
hammers, anvil, and forge.
A few feet from where I stand

rest millstones and grindstones: immortal.
In the spirit of the original,
this studio was rebuilt and placed here
in the shadow of the Pompidou,
like a footnote in the book of eternity.
I find myself quieted,
a little happier than I was an hour ago
walking in the rain on the rue Rambuteau.
The students and teacher file past.
I look at their faces,
so young. As they leave
they seem happy, too,
opening their umbrellas to the drizzle outside.
So now it's just the tools and the sculptures
and me, the only one left in the little museum
except for the uniformed guard at the entrance
and the kind lady behind her white desk.
Sitting alone, I give myself over
to the consolation of the artist's work.
Consolation is not what I came here for,
but it is better than anything I might have wanted
before I came to Paris.

Achilles Mourning the Death of Patroclus

At the Pompidou, I sit on a wooden bench,
looking at what seems to be
nothing more than a few gray scratches,
the merest idea of a painting—
a thin horizon line,
pencil marks and erasures,
the title written in charcoal in cursive in English,
and a bloodred spill of paint in the center—
Twombly's *Achilles Mourning the Death of Patroclus*.
The artist practiced painting in the dark
to unlearn the skills he'd been taught.
He said he would have liked to be Poussin.
He read and was inspired by the great poets—
Homer, Rumi, Rilke.
He said the pencil is more his medium
than paint and paintbrush.
Looking, I try to make sense of things in my notebook.
Twombly, like me, is a southerner, a Virginian.
He's nostalgic for the beauty of southern landscapes.
He thinks about the past and is interested
in ancient things, ancient places. All this I understand.
His move to Italy in the fifties—
"when Rome was like paradise"—
I can only imagine. He sought freedom,
a kind of anonymity,
and was perfectly happy to live outside the confines
of fame and the demands of New York galleries.
He cared little for the movements of his time
and did not particularly value what he'd learned
in art school. His rough white canvases
with their scrawls and scratches
remind me of my artless notebooks, also filled

with scrawls and scratches, pencil marks, erasures,
sketches, check marks,
rows of words and lines crossed out.
The blank pages of a notebook—
the sort of nothingness from which beauty springs:
the struggle to grieve a fabled hero.

Courbet

Here at the end
of the great hall
in the Musée D'Orsay,
I find five immense canvases
in a large gallery,
an eggplant-purple room,
off to the left like a chapel.
The Artist's Studio.
The Winter Hunt.
Courbet asked that we note
the blue shadows in the snow—
that, he said,
was how snow should be painted.
In *A Burial at Ornans,*
a dark parade of country folk
process from village to cemetery,
the canvas some ten feet by twenty,
its grand, heroic style
realistic. The heavy coffin
draped with a white pall
is borne by four clergymen.
The pallbearers, priests,
mourners, and bereft family
move as one. It is the moment
of the interment,
and the painter stops time
with three horizontal planes.
Across the top of the scene,
the vast empty sky of eternity
against which the holy cross
is raised, lifted by an altar boy.
In the bottom center of the canvas,

an open grave dug in the earth—
a pit devoid of light, a black abyss.
And in the large middle section,
the crowded world of the living,
mourners accompanying the dead to the grave,
offering last rites, saying prayers, comforting one another,
turning away, grieving, performing their sacred duties.

On the second floor near the Impressionist gallery
I stop in the little café.
From the ceiling's iron beams
gold bells hang and illuminate the room.
An enormous clock is a reminder
that one must make room for both wine and paintings,
nourish both body and soul
if one is to spend the balance of the afternoon
wandering the old train station turned museum,
looking and gazing and thinking
and working the mind to a fever vision.
After a light lunch of quiche, salad,
and two tall glasses of Kir Royal,
I find myself in the late afternoon, an hour before closing,
stepping into an almost hidden gallery
far from the grand Courbets,
a little temple unto itself
where I discover a small Courbet
I've never heard of or seen before.
The crudely lavish canvas
that shocked nineteenth-century Paris—
a nude woman in bed, lying on her back, legs spread—
makes my heart pump faster
and heats my cheeks to a warm pink blush—
The Origin of the World.

Dalí

In my tiny galley kitchen,
I arrange the cheese on a blue plate—
a Pouligny-Saint-Pierre
goat cheese shaped like a pyramid,
some Bleu d'Auvergne from the south,
and a bit of white-rinded Pont-l'Évêque,
a cheese that delighted
Norman monks in the Middle Ages.
In the bowl I toss a plain green salad
with watercress and herbs
to serve alongside the veal
with mushrooms and cream sauce.
I'm trying to emulate the meal
I enjoyed in a café near the Place des Vosges
on Sunday afternoon
as rain fell on the empty street.
The clock ticks loudly
as the veal sizzles in the butter.
The window is open. There's a breeze.
As I shake the copper skillet,
I sing a little to myself.
Cooking for oneself
is a special kind of feast—
the cheese and the meat fresh from the market,
and the wine, a chardonnay
thoughtfully paired with the veal
by the shop owner who climbed his ladder
to the highest shelf
as if retrieving a rare book.
I also purchased an estate Bordeaux
the wine merchant had marked down,
a wine that grows ever more delicious

as it is savored, like my loneliness,
glass by glass through the night.
Hoping no one visits this evening,
I spread the white cloth. I lay the table.
I note that in the apartment I've rented
the simple flatware is stored in two earthen vases
and arranged like flowers.
In the antique store I passed on the street today,
I noted a display of Christofle silver spoons,
standing upright and tied together
like a bouquet of sunflowers
or a sheaf of wheat.
And then yesterday at the museum in Montmartre
there was Dalí's flatware,
Dalí who sees the knife as a feather
or a snail with tears,
the spoon as a shell
or an artichoke leaf.
The long tines of the fork
are the tentacles of a squid with sapphire eyes
or the tusks of an elephant.
"The difference between me and
the surrealists," Dalí says,
suddenly standing beside me,
dropping in unexpectedly
as he is wont to do,
"is that I am a surrealist."
The artist bows as he holds my chair
and seats me at a special table
in eternity's preposterous and transcendent café,
a table for one
on a barren coast beneath a dying olive tree,
upon whose bare branch a clock is melting
like Camembert cheese.

The Golden Sphere

In the Tuileries Garden, the golden
sphere seems to float over the pond
where on summer days children sail
their miniature wooden schooners,

the pristine sails as white as clouds.
And beyond the shimmering water,
an obelisk's pointed gold pyramid
looks much like the sharp pencil-tip

with which I take notes and sketch.
Beside the obelisk, a single woman
in a stylish red coat pauses to study
the orb floating like a setting sun,

or cooly note, as a Parisian might,
the American on the other side of the pond.

Strindberg and Miller

I take pictures atop the Pompidou.
The scene is sunless and gray,
as monochromatic as black-and-whites,
the rooftops lost in the fog and foul air
that has descended upon the city this week.
Paris looks bleak and lonely,
as it must have looked to August Strindberg,
who abandoned Copenhagen and the theater
and came here
depressed, alone and fretful.
He had suffered a series of breakdowns.
He struggled with his writing,
his marriage,
and could find no solace.
He came searching and found nothing—
Paris almost did him in.
He became addicted to absinthe
and fell prey to hallucinations and paranoia.
He was looking for something
and wrote his tormented *Inferno*,
the autobiographical novel of prose poems
about delusion, neurosis, and disappointment
with chapter titles such as "Purgatory," "Hell,"
"Tribulations," and "Whither?"
And then he painted his black and blue canvas:
Night of Jealously,
conjuring his despair
as a storm, the chaotic vigor
of the brushstrokes imbued with
mad agony as well as his
longing and redemption.

Decades later,
Henry Miller came to Paris.
He read Strindberg's *Inferno*
and perfectly understood the ordeal and the agony,
"the cloud of unknowing"
that surrounded the artist.
Miller knew what it was to be "an alien soul."
Miller said, "One can live in Paris—
I discovered that!—
on just grief and anguish."
But Miller would never go mad,
never cave in to despair.
Back in Brooklyn,
Miller had suffered his own season in hell.
But in Paris,
Miller came to understand
freedom is obtained by the acceptance of suffering
and by giving suffering meaning.
He foresaw the future of poetry,
the terrible day when poets
would deliberately make themselves *unintelligible*
and renounce their power to move us.
Such poetry, he said, is worthless,
a betrayal of trust.
The world, Miller insisted,
hangs on the poet's every word;
the place of renewal is the heart, he said,
and there the poet must anchor himself.

Under the plane trees
of Montparnasse
wearing his usual khakis and white t-shirt,
Henry Miller,
a skeletal wraith

moneyless and hungry
wanders with purpose,
strolling past cafés
filled with wanton lovers,
dreaming loners,
and black-jacketed waiters who pay him no mind,
his heart feverish with the miracle of writing—
every misfortune transformed to good account.

The Gift

Last night,
walking in the Latin Quarter
and dreamily following
the narrow cobblestone passageways
wherever they led
and losing myself in the crowds
carousing outside the brightly lighted bars
and hideaway restaurants,
I saw Man Ray in a gray suit
stepping through a doorway
and up narrow stairs. The lights
went on in a second-floor apartment,
and through the sheer white curtains
I could see he was conversing
with Kiki, his model and muse.
Kiki looked fabulous
with her soulful eyes
and straight black bangs.
She was the kind of spirit
who would enchant Man Ray's famous guests,
cook for them,
woo them,
and at evening's end,
sing for them.
I thought to ring the bell
and tell Kiki
that Man Ray's photograph
of her naked back turned into a violin
is famous, that *Le Violon d'Ingres*
is now pictured on calendars
and even on the postcard
I dropped this morning

into the yellow mailbox.
I thought to tell Man Ray
that seeing his *Indestructible
Object* changed the way I look
at everything, but then realized
words can't really explain why
I embrace such a mad thing—
a metronome with a cutout of an eye
glued to the pendulum.
Suddenly the lights went out in the apartment.
I had the feeling that Kiki and Man Ray
were looking down at me,
looking up at them.
Alone in the milling crowds
of the Latin Quarter at night,
I looked for words to tell Kiki and Man Ray.
Then, as if he could hear me,
Man Ray opened the window
and leaned out.
His pomaded hair shone in the street light—
I could see the rakes of his comb.
A purple stain, perhaps of wine, bloomed on his lapel.
He asked me why I didn't ring the bell and told me
Erik Satie was with him the day he created
his first readymade—the flatiron with nails.
I told him I love the flatiron with nails.
He said it was a century ago
and he didn't speak French
and Satie didn't speak English,
but that Satie said *ce n'est pas important.*
They had been drinking hot grog—
it was winter in Paris and cold—
and they were walking to Man Ray's gallery show
and saw the iron in a shop window.

Man Ray bought the iron then and there
and with Satie searched for glue and nails.
Then Kiki too leaned out into the light,
her black bangs falling forward, her face pale, her eyes
glistening, her neck long and white against the dark room.
"He called it *Le Cadeau*"—her musical accent was charming!—
"which in English means 'the gift.'"
"I know, I know," I said, wanting to say more,
wanting to say I've known *The Gift* all my life.
Kiki asked did I know Man Ray grew up
among sewing machines and flatirons—
his father a tailor, his mother a seamstress?
I told her that's interesting. I didn't know that.
I told her my grandfather was a blacksmith.
"He made wheels, gates, and tools. I think
he actually made flatirons, too," I said.
"A godlike man who dared seize the fire,"
Man Ray said. "Yes," I said, "that's right."
I explained that my grandfather died
before I was born. My mother
was with him when his heart stopped.
"*Je suis désolée*," Kiki said. "*Je suis désolée*."
In the upstairs open window
behind the white curtains
the two of them became
darkening shadows.
Kiki and Man Ray.
Muse and artist.
Later,
walking home at midnight
on the cobblestone quais along the Seine
and looking down into the black water
and the golden lights reflected there,
I regretted that I never knew my grandfather,

never got to talk with him at his work,
the ring of the anvil, the heat of the forge.
Then I heard Kiki's voice
speaking to me as clearly as if she
and Man Ray were walking beside me.
"It doesn't matter," she said.
"It doesn't matter that you never talked.
The forge is a gift. Indestructible.
Like stories about your grandfather
and his little girl in the house practicing piano,
keeping time with the all-seeing metronome."

The Place des Vosges

In Jean-Paul Sartre's novel *Nausea*,
the hero's existential awakening takes place
on a bench beneath the boughs of chestnut trees
in a park much like the Place des Vosges.
Antoine Roquentin feels the cold shiver of nothingness
against the wild, unstoppable abundance of life
he found meaningless. But I find
the fountain and the branches in blossom
and this wooden bench bathed in bright sunshine
a place of perfect rest, a blessing, a gift,
and unbutton my coat to let my spirit breathe
and take flight in the afternoon breeze.
On the grass, on blankets scattered here and there,
people laze and lounge and laugh,
they have bread and wine,
they share stories about their dreams.
I'd say they haven't a care in the world
if I thought for a moment that was true,
but that is exactly what makes them beautiful,
weighty, and meaningful,
the way their joy transcends and surpasses suffering,
so that this existential moment
is something they celebrate, lifting full glasses
and, I'd like to think, remembering Sartre,
who believed in neither love nor joy
and wrote *nothingness, contingency, anguish,* and *nausea,*
though he also believed,
as I do, sitting with my pen and blue notebook
on a bench in the Place des Vosges,
in writing the *yes* of a poem.

The Bateau-Lavoir

The Bateau-Lavoir is gone, burned to the ground.
Nonetheless, I've come to 13 rue Ravignan
to sit on the bench in the cobblestone park
and pay homage to the lost, ramshackle,
poorly lit studios of Picasso and Braque,
Matisse, Apollinaire, and Kees van Dongen.
There's nothing here to see,
no cold room to stand in
imagining Jean Cocteau at his desk
or Modigliani at his easel with his model.
On a light-dappled bench by a Wallace fountain,
I linger beneath the chestnut trees
a little lost, a little disappointed.
In my coat pocket,
I've a half-baguette from Miss Manon.
It's noon. After an interlude
in which unbidden thoughts flow tranquilly through my mind
like a thousand richly painted clouds,
I rise from the bench,
cup my hands and sip from the fountain,
splash water on my face,
and then stroll the lanes to the square atop Montmartre.

In the Place du Tertre
I find artists selling work,
sketching portraits and painting *en plein air,*
everyone enjoying the day and the warm spring sun.
I nibble my baguette and observe the portraitists at work,
the skill, virtuosity, and cleverness
apparent in every charcoal likeness.
If my daughter were here
I'd ask if she would sit for a portrait,

just for me.
Then I remember:
earlier today,
down the hill from the Bateau-Lavoir,
I saw a man my age alone in his shop,
painting on a small wood panel
dead game birds and cut lilies,
a still life worthy of a Dutch master.
And this morning in the metro
I heard a sax player who played Sidney Bechet
like Sidney Bechet.
And when I changed trains at Concorde
I heard a violinist playing
"The Lark Ascending,"
the trills and squeaks
sending birdsong through the tunnels.
A year or two back,
I read a story about Joshua Bell,
the American violinist.
One morning in the DC metro,
with a violin made by Stradivari in 1713,
Bell played six classical masterpieces,
one after another,
beginning with Bach's Chaconne.
The stale air in the pedestrian arcade came alive.
The dust motes sparkled.
With the tiny instrument
the artist made music Brahms called
"a whole world of the deepest thoughts
and most powerful feelings."
But that day in the subway—
and here's what's hard to understand—
no one even stopped to listen.

Cathedral

Saint-Eustache

Songbirds live
in the old cathedral,
caged birds bought at the street market
and freed as a kind of offering.
Now doves and finches and parakeets
nest in the crooks of the nave's highest arches,
roosting on the impossibly high
sills of stained-glass windows,
looking down into the valley of the altar
as if from cliffs.

Twice a day, the birds will sing:
at dawn
when the blue light
of angels' wings
and the yellow light of halos
flood into their nests to wake them,
and during mass,
when the organ fills
the valley below with thunder.
These birds love thunder,
never having seen a drop of rain.
They love it when the people below stand up
and sing. They fly
in mad little loops
from window to window,
from the tops of the arches
down toward the candles and tombs,
making the sign of the cross.

When I look up during mass
to the world's light falling
through the arms of saints,
I see birds flying
through blue columns of incense
as if it were simple wood smoke
rising from a cabin's chimney
in a remote and hushed forest.

George Whitman

The photographer Henri Cartier-Bresson
tried to capture what he called
"the decisive moment,"
photographing landscapes
in which human beings
seemed incidental,
though never placed entirely by accident.
Walking along the Seine,
taking pictures of everything,
I feel lucky
just to embrace the *in*decisive moments—
paving stones, rooftops, trees in bloom, scooters.
In the stalls of the *bouquinistes*
I find all I could want:
a copy of *Alcools* by Apollinaire,
a volume of Reverdy,
a collection of French novels bound in red leather.
I ask permission and take a picture,
the books as beautiful
as the bouquet of flowers Renoir painted
a hundred years ago
that stopped me in my tracks
yesterday in the museum.
The *bouquiniste*,
face weathered and craggy,
invites me to take all the pictures I want.
Cartier-Bresson's photographs are framed
on the walls of museums,
documenting the poetry of the moment,
but my photographs
are like images from a dream
that no one on earth could make sense of,

maybe not even me.
A teacup and spoon.
A pilgrim's seashell.
The blue Paris sky.
Still, I know the photograph of the red books
will one day hang framed in my study
in honor of the *bouquiniste.*
If I were Cartier-Bresson,
I'd take photographs of all the *bouquinistes,*
portraits of the booksellers
before the booksellers vanish.
I stroll across the bridge
to Shakespeare and Company.
It seems a thousand years ago
George Whitman offered me a bed
in the bookstore's upstairs room,
a room I would share
with a beautiful stranger from Kyoto.
Whitman believed in kindness,
as I do, and I remember
how the woman and I sat in silence
among the walls of books
while afternoon light
poured through the windows—
shafts of arrows.

Surrealism

Maillol's twenty bold women
in the boxwood gardens of the Tuileries,
Winged Victory crying "Freedom!" in the Louvre,
an unnamed robed beauty weeping
over a grave at Père Lachaise—
these are the teachers of my senses,
these figures in stone, marble, and bronze.
And so now it is natural, almost inevitable
as I walk past the shop windows,
to take note of the mannequins, too,
those wooden figures behind the glass.
In Paris I've seen mannequins painted gold,
like the street mimes with gold faces and clothes
who stand in the Latin Quarter on pedestals
like statues, as still as a mannequin in a window.
On boulevard Saint-Michel I saw mannequins
whose faces were covered in black bags,
and on the rue de Rivoli, mannequins
carrying their wooden heads in their hands
like Saint Denis at Sacré-Cœur.
Female mannequins have long, elegant necks.
Child mannequins sometimes have lights
glowing inside their hollowed bodies.
Articulated mannequins move, like puppets—
a tuxedoed mannequin leaps over a black-paper puddle.
On avenue Montaigne, I stood outside a men's store
eating a strawberry tart.
I gazed at a mannequin's head imprisoned in a birdcage
and thought of 1938
and the Exposition Internationale du Surréalisme,
when all the surrealists presented mannequins—
one with its wooden head trapped in a birdcage!

The surrealists loved mannequins,
their silence and mystery.
Magritte painted a wooden head sky blue
with clouds drifting across the face
and called it *The Future of Statues*.
Man Ray adorned faces with glass tears;
Dalí covered bodies with spoons and butterflies.
Marcel Duchamp, Max Ernst, Yves Tanguy, and Joan Miró
saw in mannequins the soul of humankind—
mute sexual longings,
subconscious urges,
all our taboos concealed and exposed.
After the 1938 exhibition,
the surrealists immediately returned all the mannequins
to the stores from which they had been borrowed,
the artworks transformed back into ordinary objects,
the most surreal gesture of all.

"The Drunken Boat"

This morning on the rue Férou,
I found myself caught unawares
by "Le Bateau ivre"—
Arthur Rimbaud's poem
carved on a wall that runs the length of the lane.
In the narrow cobblestone street
I translated the first lines into the air
then stepped aside
to let a bicycle rattle past.
The bicycle woke me to the fact
I was walking Saint-Germain's winding streets
a little bit like a drunken boat myself,
adrift on a sea of reveries.
Ahead I could see the spires of Saint-Sulpice
and over my shoulder the Luxembourg Gardens.
I walked the empty lane a few slow steps at a time,
gazing up at the poem,
deliberating.

When I was young
I carried Rimbaud's poems
like a talisman in my coat pocket,
finding in him a visionary comrade
and in the drunken boat's desire to be free
hope for my own future.
La vraie vie est absente, he said.
He thought the real, true life
was absent, that we aren't really
a part of this world. At nineteen,
Rimbaud gave up writing,
left France for the West Indies and Africa,
became a soldier, a deserter,

ran guns in Ethiopia,
had his leg amputated
and died at forty, a penniless businessman.
His letters describe life without poetry or love:
desperate, wretched, preposterous, gloomy.
Hélas! que notre vie est donc misérable!
"Alas! That life should be so miserable!"

Toward the end of the lane,
on the other side of the wall, above the poem,
cherry trees were coming into bloom,
pink and white branches reaching into the sky.
Perhaps because of the generous light
and the delicate blossoms
the poem's final image moved me—
a sad child at twilight
squatting by a cold black puddle
and releasing a toy boat
frêle comme un papillon de mai—
"as fragile as a May butterfly."
There at the wall
I had to finally acknowledge—
I must have repressed it when I was younger—
that Rimbaud the man was never free,
never happy or loved,
never content
to be a little boat bobbing about
on a sun-drenched, windswept sea.
I tried to feel the poem as I did when I was a teenager,
tried to catch the fire that meant so much
when life seemed overwhelming
and I was breaking.
I remembered the photograph
I've kept on my desk over the years—

the boy's chaste white blouse, the angelic face.
I reached out and ran my hand over the wall's carved letters,
a wistful reminder of youth's bright hopes
and bottomless despair.

And now, sitting here
in my apartment at midnight
writing in my diary
and sipping wine
by a tall window opened to song and laughter,
I find myself describing the rue Férou,
Rimbaud the seer,
and the contrast of his reality.
Then I remember the moment
the bicycle and rider rattled past
over the bumpy cobblestones,
the Frenchman in his tweed jacket
half smiling,
his jaunty cap and sunglasses,
the books and bread in his basket bouncing.
"Maybe," I write, "I could be
like him, the man on the bike,
more or less content at the end of the day,"
and then I imagine
the rider lying on a sofa
in a small apartment and reading by lamplight,
a Paris moon in the window,
a bicycle leaning
by the door in the shadowed courtyard.

Letter to a Friend

You would like it here.
From my apartment on rue Saint-Paul
it's only a few minutes' walk
through the labyrinthine old village
past the brocante shops and galleries
to the Bibliothèque Forney.
The guarded medieval gates once opened
for the archbishop's horse and carriage;
now at the librarian's desk
an identification card with my picture
swiped through an electronic sensor
opens the door to the courtyard,
where I take a moment to look up
and admire the ancient walls
of golden stone and the bright red windows,
iron balconies, and black towers.
Stone steps built in the 1400s
climb up to the library
devoted to the decorative arts—
the stacks rich with books
on painting, architecture, and design.
You'd find it a good place to work.
The reading room has the feel of a monastery,
yet at the long library tables
stylish young people tap away on laptops.
On the other side of the stacks
I find a small desk by a mullioned window
and lose myself
in a book of Brassaï photographs.
I intently study a portrait of Picasso in his studio,
the look in his eyes. I turn the page
and find old Paris graffiti—

names and faces
scratched and carved into walls.
Brassaï titled his photos after the image—
The Magician, Masks and Faces, The Sun King.
He called this "the language of the wall,"
fugitive souls with knives
cutting their innermost visions
into centuries-old stone.
I turn the page: a pair of initials
inside a heart.
Eternity
and the timelessness of desire.
I turn the page again and find *Death*—
a carved skull, the empty eyes—
and think of the scholar's skull,
the memento mori.
This morning I climbed the spiral stone stairway
to pore over these images from the past
and lose myself in thought,
and now—
sitting by the window,
happy in the window light—
I am as absorbed by the photographs
of carved skulls and lovers' hearts
as if they were sacred scripture
illuminated in blue and gold
by the meticulous brushwork of monks of old
and I a young novitiate
tracing the text with my fingertips
and reading by candlelight.
I share this with you
because I know you know what I mean.

Sonnet

Quai des Célestins, the Seine flowing fast
beneath the Pont Marie—turbulent, wild,
gold-green—a sure sign spring is coming.

Hemingway's flat on the rue du Cardinal-Lemoine:
two small rooms, no hot water, no toilet.
He was happy then, living there and writing.

Bronze nudes in the Tuileries, all by Maillot.
His museum was founded by one of his models.
Which one is she, here in the boxwood maze?

In the evening, rain shines mystically
as it falls through the streetlamps. Streetlamps
light the way, one after the other, home.

Redon wanted his paintings to lift the veils of enigma.
When I come to Paris, I live on bread and wine.

Gustave Moreau

The painter turned his home
into a museum, which opened after his death:
tiny rooms
thick with his furniture, books,
and objet d'arts. On every silk-covered wall
crowds of framed chalk sketches reach
to the ceiling's belle epoque crown molding.
Tapestries, chairs with bullion fringes,
chevron floors, cane patterns on chairs,
the china collection,
a bookcase with three busts on top,
a shelf crammed with small white statues
and a host of black pitchers.
In his bedroom, attached to his narrow single bed,
a chess table—
pawns, kings, and queens in position—
and another table awaiting its silver tray
with tea or wine.
Imagine living that way,
the things you love most
always at the ready, visible to the eye.
The painter added two floors atop his house:
the extravagant studio
with paneled walls and high ceilings.
The studio now displays the grand canvases—
scenes from the Bible—
Moses Saved from the Waters,
The Apparition of John the Baptist—
alongside myths the artist makes even stranger—
Ulysses on his voyage home,
Prometheus on the mountaintop,
a Thracian girl

carrying the head of Orpheus on his lyre.
In *À rebours*
Huysmans astutely wrote
"Moreau was a pupil of no man,"
a painter "without provable ancestors,
without possible descendants."
It's true—
at the École des Beaux-Arts,
his students included young Matisse and Rouault,
who paint nothing like him.
I'm told Moreau loved a woman he called his "only friend"
but never married. Instead,
the artist lived with and cared for his parents
until their deaths, after which
he remained alone. Before he died,
Moreau arranged the museum
and hung his most ideal, most magical paintings
next to unfinished work,
outlines and sketches of would-be masterpieces,
the oil paint never to be applied
a reminder that life is fleeting
and every moment of utmost value,
that in our numbered days
we will never finish
all the work we are put here to do.

Christic in the Garden of Olives

Only steps from the apartment,
I steal down the alley
and through the red side-doors of the church
to meditate once more on Delacroix's altarpiece.

My wooden chair leans back against a stone column.
Under the crossing's high dome,
candles flicker like stars through the olive trees.
Lord, how many days have I come here

to be with your sleeping disciples
and the three angels hovering in the darkness?
And why did it take me so long to see
you are not waiting for the soldiers

with their torches and weapons to arrest you,
not waiting for Pilate to condemn you?
Already you are lifting your arms
to the executioner's hammer and nails.

Tin Cups

Across from the Saint-Paul station
I fill my water bottle at a Wallace fountain.
Here on the rue Saint-Antoine,
I rest my hand on Charity's slipper
and drink until my thirst is quenched.
As I disappear down the steps of the metro,
I remember that from the fountain's side
tin cups once hung—
tin cups so that anyone may drink.

Existential

1. *The Existential Poem*

We ordered *deux cafés* and the waiter left.
(She'd rung my apartment in the Marais,
said it was an emergency,
said meet at the café on the rue des Barres.)
Then she took from its envelope
the love letter an acquaintance she hardly knew had mailed her—
French written in ink on blue paper—
and asked me to help translate
into English—

> *J'attendrai—*

> *I will wait for you*
> *beyond the waves of sorrow…*

2. *The Existential Answer*

Did the pimp who stabbed
young Samuel Beckett one night in Paris
understand he was fated
to convey the existential answer?
The pimp's name was Prudent.
When Beckett got out of the hospital—
the knife had just missed his heart and lung—
he visited the jail
and asked the Frenchman why he'd done it.
"Je ne sais pas, monsieur.
Je ne sais pas."

3. *The Existential Question*

"Where are the souls
of the great French writers?
Where is Victor Hugo?
Down what alley do the shadows
of Rimbaud and Verlaine disappear?
Beautiful language like a kiss,
upon whose lips do you now become
even more beautiful,
plus chaste?"
asked the old *bouquiniste*
as she closed and locked
the heavy doors of her wooden bookstall.

Aura

In Paris people have a funny habit
of telling me what I should write.

Usually it's something they see—
an oddly glowing angle of light

along the stone wall of the rue Férou
or the iridescent wake of a barge

striking Pont Neuf's stone arches,
the silky length of the Seine agleam.

Waiting at the Saint-Paul station
or daydreaming in Saint-Sulpice,

acquaintances tap my shoulder and say
instead of another painting they'd prefer

the numinous poetry that exists
outside the frame—the radiant aura.

An aura, in fact, is what the people
would really like to see from poems—

not just the day's complaint.
Paris asks not for chiaroscuro

but halo-light—the miraculous,
golden yellow, resplendent aura.

When I linger in a café over coffee
or wait in line for the morning's baguette,

people I've never met tell me
poetry needs more soul, more feeling.

"We want auras in poems," Paris tells me.
"Auras and light, and we want them now."

Redouté

At the Luxembourg Museum
I see a watercolor of a rose
by Redouté,
the celebrated painter of flowers.
I'm at the Josephine exhibit,
discovering the life of Napoléon's wife.
Her famed gardens
and her rare cultivars of roses
could only be immortalized,
I am told
by the voice in my headphones,
by such a one as Redouté,
known in his day
as "the Raphael of flowers."
In the artist's lifetime he published
two botanical books,
famous and coveted to this day,
sumptuous collections of his watercolors.
The voice in the headphones
drifts away
and I'm no longer in Paris
but a child in the home of my aunt Ila,
her small Carolina house
with teardrop chandeliers
like Josephine's in Versailles.
I'm in the formal living room—
the off-limits room reserved for wakes
and visits from the pastor—
furnished with the frozen elegance
of French provincial tables,
sofa, lamps, and high-backed chairs
no one was allowed to sit in.

I've slipped into the room
to steal some hard candy
from the cut-glass bowl
and find myself staring at
Redouté's flowering jasmine,
a cherry drop melting in my cheek.
In the Luxembourg Museum
I realize that as a boy
in the homes of all my southern aunts—
Opal, Ruby, Mable, Marie, Blake,
and Martha—
I saw Redouté's flowers
framed and hanging in those southern rooms
as if in the stillness of museums—
the delicate and meticulous roses,
tulips,
camellias, and pansies.

The French Word for "Sky"

Tilting my head and looking up
at the Louvre's ceilings,
I gaze at the work
of Louis Le Vau and Charles Le Brun,
then walk the palace's rooms
trying to decide which ceiling I love more,
Delacroix's *Apollo Slays Python*
or Georges Braque's doves?
In the Salle des Bronzes,
Cy Twombly's ceiling is blue,
a hue I'd never have imagined
for the Louvre. To make a sky
there are many blues,
but this is Mediterranean blue—
eternal blue of the Greek gods
and light-drenched sea and sky.
And there is a yellow sun
and red and green planets
that I'd like to think even I could have painted,
and I am reminded how
when I was a young father
my little study,
lined with tall bookshelves,
became the baby's crib room.
I painted the ceiling blue—
the French word for "sky" is *ciel*—
and pasted plastic stars there,
little stars that shone
when I turned out the lights
and kissed my child.
Some nights I'd lie on the floor
next to my son in the dark,

stargazing, thinking
about palaces and crib rooms
and how deeply we love
ceilings fretted with stars.
Lying on the floor
and listening to Andrew babble and coo,
I felt like Napoléon in his palace bed
peering up at painted tempest clouds torn apart
and revealing the glory of heaven,
the gilded ceiling crowded
with cherubim and red-winged seraphim,
a host of golden angels
keeping watch over the household
while the tired emperor closed his eyes
and dreamed extravagant and marvelous dreams.

The Water Lilies: Green Reflections

I'm sitting before Monet's *Nymphéas: Reflets vert.*
The tiniest brushstroke of viridian pigment
textures the water like shot silk.
A woman in a blue kimono
with a black obi knotted at her back
glides dream-like through the Orangerie.
When she sits next to me on the bench
beneath the gauze-covered oval skylight,
I think of Ryōkan's poem—
> *Oh that my monk's robe*
> *were wide enough*
> *to gather up all the suffering people*
> *in this floating world—*

a poem I think Monet would have liked,
maybe even would have whispered under his breath
when he rose before blue-black dawn
and carried easel, canvas, and paint box
through the dark to his lily pond.
And now—
her embroidered silk sleeve alongside my old tweed coat—
drooping willow branches calm the purple water.
The green of the lilies deepens.
The shadows darken.
I'd like to ask Ryōkan
what brought the woman here this moment
that together we might imagine the bright clouds and breezes
blowing through the garden at Giverny.
Then I remember another poem the monk wrote
with his brush on a paper kite:
> *heaven-up-great-wind.*

At the Carnavalet and the Cognacq-Jay

I show my late father Voltaire's writing chair—
comfortable, not too big or soft,
resting on curved legs with tiny wheels
and brilliantly rigged with two
pivoting mechanical iron arms,
one holding a reading panel
for manuscripts, the other
a desk with drawers for ink and pens.
I could live in that chair
for the rest of my life,
I tell my father,
then show him Proust's room—
the cork-lined walls,
the tiny bed of dreams,
the drop-leaf rosewood writing desk
where the novelist built
a "cathedral of words."
I point out the lamp with its green shade,
the hardback notebooks
on the nightstand.
I tell him Proust's handwriting
was nearly as bad as mine,
and he says
that's because writing flows like rapids,
not like something printed or typed.
My father invites me to look at Napoléon's
mahogany campaign box
with its "necessaries"—
crystal glasses, silver razor,
ebony vials of cologne,
gold mirror, ivory snuffbox.
Fancier, he says,

than what he was used to,
back when he was a soldier in battle.
I look at his eyes, so blue.
When I was growing up in Virginia,
he regaled me
with a thousand war stories,
more about comrades and travel
than dying and battle
—stories I still remember verbatim today.
My father let his life bear witness—
the courtesy of his tested heart,
the tears and kindness.
If only in that, I pray we are the same.
As we descend the winding staircase
beneath the Carnavalet's chandeliers
he asks am I hungry.
We walk two blocks
to a bistro for lunch.
We've already eaten there three times this week,
and from the menu today
we ask for escargots,
rabbit leg, steak tartare,
lamb with herbs, duck confit
—unlike the soup he typically ordered,
so harsh were his lessons from the Depression.
We devour huge bowls of chocolate mousse,
and over coffee
he asks about my sabbatical, do I miss my family.
I love Paris,
but it's hard being so far from Laura.
And I miss the children—
their laughter and wisdom.
He says he felt the same,
all those air-force years he was away,

flying around the world,
his military life so far from us.
We touch our glasses
of eaux-de-vie—
I'm drinking plum, he's sipping pear—
and smile at the paradoxical truth:
even now, knowing what we know,
neither of us wants to leave the Marais
and go home. After lunch we walk
down rue Elzévir to the Cognacq-Jay,
where my father grows rhapsodic
over the Canaletto paintings of the Grand Canal.
My father's been everywhere,
but never to Venice, city of dreams.
In his honeyed southern voice
he tells me Venice looks very different
from where he lives now.
I tell him maybe we could
book an overnight train
and go there.
We could sleep
in the narrow bunks,
like soldiers in army cots.
His posture changes.
"Maybe," he says.
He leans closer to the Canaletto and the canal,
almost touching the canvas with his nose
to see the master's brushstrokes,
light on water
and royal palaces,
the black gondolas,
sky,
and majestic clouds.
My father and I

didn't talk like this when
we were younger and he was alive—
we were too different;
but now we talk all the time,
and understand each other perfectly.

Pont des Arts

The pain passes,
           but the beauty remains.
                    —Renoir

Wandering the Musée de l'Orangerie with my sister,
we find a bouquet of roses painted in 1878 by Pierre-Auguste
Renoir, voluptuous white roses placed on a red velvet chair.
My sister says Renoir's last word was "flowers"
and that toward the end of his life he said of painting,
"I think I am beginning to understand something about it."
His quest for beauty was relentless, tireless,
though when painting flowers, she says,
his mind was always calm, restful, and full of good cheer.
I imagine his final year—the brushes lashed to his wrists;
the wheelchair and the makeshift sedan with bamboo poles
on which he was lifted and carried through the Louvre
so he could see the hallowed galleries one last time.
Bouquet dans une loge—so beautiful, I rub my eyes.

*

Sitting in the sun on the steps of the Palais Garnier,
my sister holds out her cellphone to show me a Degas—
the light gracing a girl, a ballerina in a yellow tutu.
She says the ballet originated with men in the royal courts,
courtiers who executed deep, elegant bows to the king,
and that young women like Degas's little girls
(who always remind me of my golden-haired daughter)
did not perform until the time of the Revolution,
when the ballet at last became a revelation
of what the body is born and made for—
a dance that moves to the music of time.

"Which," my sister says, leaning back on the opera's
warm stone steps to get the sun on her face,
"*is* the golden light—the yellow light in the Degas painting."

*

The day is filled with light, so like two pilgrims
we walk to the Seine and linger on Pont des Arts,
the bridge where ten thousand gold and silver locks
inscribed with names and fastened to the grillwork
flash and gleam, symbols of undying love;
below, the emerald water is swiftly flowing.
For a moment in time among the love locks,
the two of us lean against the black rail,
poised between heaven and earth.
Locks and wishes. Perhaps the river
makes my sister think about her son.
I find myself pondering locks
that have been broken, discarded,
divorce and death, the faded memories.

*

Outside Église Saint-Eustache,
L'Écoute—sculpture of a giant head
with hand cupped to its ear—
hears our footsteps and knows we're coming,
but because its eyes are closed it doesn't see us
when we take its portrait with our cameras.
The church's massive wooden doors swing open
and in a dark niche, a bright triptych by Keith Haring
proclaims the Lord's birth, life, and death,
the story etched into a panel of gold.
Compared to its impressive baroque neighbor,

Peter Paul Rubens's *The Disciples of Emmaus*,
the Haring is so simply drawn it seems, my sister says,
created by the hand of a child, innocent and full of faith.

*

In Saint-Paul–Saint-Louis my sister talks about her son,
the way his golden hair would fall straight down
when he hung upside down in his tire swing,
a silly smile crinkling his eyes. She relives
the day her five-year-old drowned in the river,
the river behind her house that still flows each day,
as timeless as the Seine. Each day in this church,
we find ourselves drawn to the blue prayer candles
lighted by those who came before us and still flickering.
Our fingertips touch the holy water in the pilgrim's shell.
Love and loss are something my sister knows about,
the way Renoir knew a little something about beauty.
She says pain and grief are omnipresent,
yet somehow love and loss have been spun into gold.

*

Open-eyed in the dark on the sleep-sofa, I consider
knocking on the bedroom door and waking my sister
to ask whether she thinks we'll see Renoir's roses in heaven—
a silly question that worries me and keeps me awake.
Next morning I'm still drowsing when her key rattles
the antique lock, opens the door, and the early chill
lingering on her coat is carried into the apartment.
The sweet aroma of fresh baguettes from Miss Manon
stirs my imagination and the burbling coffeemaker
opens my eyes and calls me to new adventures.
On the kitchen table a tin pot of roses from the Bastille,

the powder on the petals calm and full of good cheer
and "with whose sweet smell," my sister says, quoting Shakespeare,
"the air shall be perfumed—"

Notre-Dame

My daughter and I traveled without our family,
visiting the week before the church burned.
We stayed in a good hotel on the Left Bank
and walked everywhere—Deyrolle, Ladurée—
all the places a father wants his daughter to see.
We spent a morning in the church. Sarah told
the story of Joan of Arc, the French heroine burned
at the stake by the English at the age of nineteen.
We lit a candle beneath her monument.
After we came home Palm Sunday, I told friends
if our Paris trip could have been any sweeter,
I didn't know how. Then, when the news came,
with images of the conflagration and the spire collapsing,
Sarah found me taking sanctuary in my study.
She had her phone and showed me a picture—
the floor of the nave in ruins with piles
of charred roof beams, ashes, and broken stones.
"But look," she said, "the altar's gold cross still stands."
She quickly took the phone back and asked
if I knew the French word *apicultrices.*
She told me it's the word for beekeepers,
and beekeepers maintained colonies of bees
on the roof of Notre-Dame! "The honey of
the Holy Spirit?" I asked. She said honeybees
thrive on many roofs in Paris and showed me
the old train station of the Musée d'Orsay,
the gilded dome of the Opéra Garnier,
and even the glass roof of the Grand Palais.
The wrath of the fire could not be stopped
and the flames roared, but the thick, black smoke
simply made the bees drunk and sleepy. When
they awoke, it was a new day, and the bees were alive.

Atget

When after a sleepless night
I venture out before the sun comes up,
the empty streets
remind me of Atget's photographs,

his *vieux* Paris—the "old Paris"—
of abandoned alleyways and steep staircases
that so enthralled the surrealists.
The surrealists understood the photograph

alone could capture the essence of mystery,
its presence and its absence.
When at dawn like a ghost
I pass through the empty square at the Bastille,

I imagine the crowd gathering at noon
and looking up through their viewing glasses
at a solar eclipse. The photograph
shows everyone gazing into the day-dark sky

as if waiting for the moon
to speak a miraculous revelation in French—
"Le ciel t'aime,
le soleil connaît ton nom—"

The Left Bank

This morning I took a walk
through the Luxembourg Gardens
and saw old men
playing chess under the spring sycamores
and children
riding ponies on the paths—
like heaven, I thought.
Then at noon as church bells rang
I sat in Saint-Sulpice
and considered the Delacroix painting
of Jacob
wrestling the angel.
For the rest of the afternoon
I strolled aimlessly,
going where the wind blew,
dreaming about love and happiness.
I walked past the locked doors
of apartment buildings
once home to Hemingway
and Gertrude Stein,
Man Ray
and Henry Miller,
and the fact I was lost
and could remember none of the fabled addresses
deepened
the sense of mystery of each street corner
and alley, the feelings of loss
and thoughts of what might have been.
I wondered where de Chirico lived.
Maybe on the rue Saint-André des Arts?
I wondered if Modigliani lived
in that apartment up there,

the one with the geraniums in the window box.
Some people say that painting is dead.
Some people say
there will never be another golden age.
Maybe that's why little things can be so moving,
little things in a shop window—
red roses in a blue vase,
a yellow-faced wooden clock,
a bent piece of brown wire like a twisted vine
holding glass grapes
the color of Prosecco and Merlot.
As I was walking I told myself,
"Let's go to Deyrolle,
say hello to the tigers and butterflies
and chat awhile with the gardener prince."
Nearby—I was glad to remember!—
there's an alley I love,
tiny and dark,
which makes me feel fully imagined
and written,
like a character in a Diderot novel.
But when I looked up,
I saw "Le Bateau ivre"
and realized I was on the rue Férou again—
the third time this week—
and that I'd walked Saint-Germain-des-Prés
in some sort of crazy circle
as I daydreamed.
That's okay. You go to no place accidentally.
George Bellows said you can learn more
from painting one street scene—
if that's what I've been doing in my head—
than from six months in an atelier.
I once saw a Man Ray painting of the rue Férou,

a lovely, calm picture
so atypically quiet and subdued for the surrealist
that it seemed to me it could've been painted
by my aunt Grace, back in Carolina.
Her brush was lively.
She would have loved Paris,
drinking tea at the Café de Flore
and reasoning with the existentialists.
Grace is gone now.
The relatives back in Carolina
say she's in heaven,
which Laura with a sly smile once said
just might be as nice as Paris, who knows?
I'm hoping heaven is like my apartment
on the Right Bank in Saint-Paul,
with the dirty dishes piled in the sink.
When evening fell over the rooftops
I found myself leaning against the fountain
of Saint Michael, thanking him
for slaying the dragon and vanquishing evil.
Then I walked home across the Seine
by way of Pont Marie,
thinking about my desk and lamp
as the French sun set
and the lights came on
like a soft hand touching my cheek.

About the Author

Richard Jones is the author of numerous books of poetry, including *Country of Air, The Blessing: New and Selected Poems, Apropos of Nothing, Stranger on Earth,* and *Avalon.* He is also the award-winning editor of *Poetry East* and over the last four decades has curated its many anthologies, such as *The Last Believer in Words, Bliss, Origins, Wider than the Sky,* and *London.* A frequent sojourner in Paris, he lives in Illinois with his family.

TEBOT BACH
A 501 (c) (3) Literary Arts Education Non Profit

THE TEBOT BACH MISSION: advancing literacy, strengthening
community, and transforming life experiences with the power of poetry
through readings, workshops, and publications.

THE TEBOT BACH PROGRAMS
1. A poetry reading and writing workshop series for venues such as homeless
shelters, battered women's shelters, nursing homes, senior citizen daycare
centers, Veterans organizations, hospitals, AIDS hospices, correctional
facilities which serve under-represented populations. Participating poets
include: John Balaban, Brendan Constantine, Megan Doherty, Richard Jones,
Dorianne Laux, M.L. Leibler, Laurence Lieberman, Carol Moldaw, Patricia
Smith, Arthur Sze, Carine Topal, Cecilia Woloch.

2. A poetry reading and writing workshop series for the community Southern
California at large, and for schools K-University. The workshops feature
local, national, and international teaching poets; David St. John, Charles
Webb, Wanda Coleman, Amy Gerstler, Patricia Smith, Holly Prado, Dorothy
Lux, Rebecca Seiferle, Suzanne Lummis, Michael Datcher, B.H. Fairchild,
Cecilia Woloch, Chris Abani, Laurel Ann Bogen, Sam Hamill, David Lehman,
Christopher Buckley, Mark Doty.

3. A publishing component to give local, national, and international poets a
venue for publishing and distribution.

Tebot Bach
Box 7887
Huntington Beach, CA 92615-7887
714-968-0905
www.tebotbach.org